Welcome To Scotland

The Scottish National Emblem is the Thistle.

Jig and Jag have been chosen from the thousands of Thistles who applied to present this puzzle book.
There are wordsearches, wordgrids, Spot-the-difference and loads of different types of puzzles for you to try.

Good Luck

HOP ON BOARD!

JAGGY AIRWAYS

wibble McWobble

WAIT FOR ME!

THE SCOTTISH PUZZLE BOOK

Text and Illustrations
copyright © David Gall and Douglas Strachan
Jig & Jag © Gall & Strachan

First published in paperback in Great Britain 2006

Design – Douglas Strachan
Reprographics – GWP Graphics
Printing – Printer Trento, Italy

Published by

Publishing

GW Publishing
PO Box 6091
Thatcham
Berks
RG19 8XZ

Tel +44 (0) 1635 268080

www.gwpublishing.com

ISBN 09551564-3-2
978-09551564-3-4

BLUE ZONE

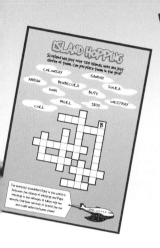

ISLAND HOPPING

Scotland has just over 790 islands, here are just eleven of them. Can you place them in the grid?

COLONSAY
ARRAN
BENBECULA
SANDAY
IONA
BUTE
FOULA
COLL
MULL
SKYE
WESTRAY

SCOTS WORDS

Here is a list of twelve Scots words and their meanings. Try and find the Scots words in the grid below.

BAIRN — child
BUNNET — soft flat hat
DROOKIT — wet
DUNT — knock against
TATTIE — potato
BRAW — fine
LOCH — lake
BRIG — bridge
GREET — weep
TREWS — tartan trousers
LASSIE — girl
KEN — know

YE AULD SCOTTISH WORDSEARCH

The words are either Down or Across

SCRAMBLED EGGS

Match up the eggs in pairs to complete the names of five creatures.

ROW
CAN
FIN
CON
TURE
SPAR
PELI
PUF
FAL
VUL

What are the missing numbers on the post?

OUR PUZZLE BOOK HAS BEEN SPLIT INTO TWO LEVELS. LEVEL 1 IS THE BLUE ZONE WHERE THE PUZZLES ARE NOT TOO DIFFICULT...

RED ZONE

TOWN TOURS

CAN YOU FIND THE FOURTEEN SCOTTISH TOWNS ON THE WINDOWS IN THE GRID?

The names can be Down, Across or Diagonal

THISTLE TOURS

TRIPLE SNAP

There are twelve cards below, each with two letters. Find four sets of three matching cards and arrange each group of six letters to spell four words.

1) _ _ _ _ _ _   2) _ _ _ _ _ _
3) _ _ _ _ _ _   4) _ _ _ _ _ _

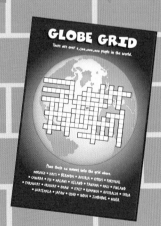

GLOBE GRID

There are over 6,300,000,000 people in the world.

Place these as named into the grid above.

MOROCCO • HAITI • BERMUDA • AUSTRIA • CYPRUS • PORTUGAL • CANADA • FIJI • MALAWI • ICELAND • PANAMA • MALI • FINLAND • PARAGUAY • URUGUAY • OMAN • ITALY • ROMANIA • AUSTRALIA • SYRIA • GUATEMALA • JAPAN • USSR • INDIA • ZIMBABWE • NIGER

...AND LEVEL 2, THE RED ZONE, WHERE THE PUZZLES CAN BE BAMBOOZLING!

PUZZLES FOR EVERYONE →

I'LL HELP YOU!

FIND THE PASSWORD

Jig wants to log into a puzzle website, but can't remember the password. You can help!

1) There are thirty letters of the alphabet on Screen One.

2) Find the four extra letters of the alphabet and arrange them to spell a word connected with Scotland.

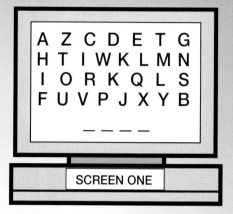

```
A Z C D E T G
H T I W K L M N
I O R K Q L S
F U V P J X Y B
_ _ _ _
```

SCREEN ONE

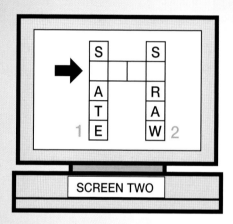

```
    S       S
→ [ ][ ][ ][ ]
    A       R
    T       A
  1 E       W 2
```

SCREEN TWO

3) Place the word into the grid on Screen Two, this will reveal two words.

4) Place the two words into the grid on Screen Three to reveal a five-letter word.

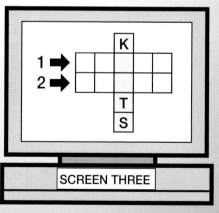

```
          K
1 → [ ][ ][ ][ ]
2 → [ ][ ][ ][ ]
          T
          S
```

SCREEN THREE

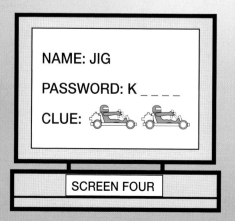

NAME: JIG

PASSWORD: K _ _ _ _

CLUE:

SCREEN FOUR

WHAT WAS THAT PASSWORD AGAIN?

A MAZE 'N SCOTLAND

Can you find a way to DUMFRIES from JOHN O'GROATS avoiding the five cities?

MOUNTAIN

Can you find these eight Scottish mountains in the grid?

LOCHNAGAR

CAIRN GORM

BEN NEVIS

BEN MACDUI

BEN AVON

AM BODACH

BEN NEVIS IS 1,343m (4,406ft) high.

CAIRN TOUL

AONACH MOR

		L	V				
	P	C	S	U			
	B	A	X	T			
N	D	E	I	L	Y	R	M
B	V	S	C	R	Q	N	T	U	N
T	E	Q	R	P	N	L	Y	P	V	L	A
D	U	N	M	O	N	T	X	P	L	B	O	V	T
T	R	M	N	J	R	M	O	V	W	B	J	C	M	A	R
K	J	O	E	T	U	P	U	Y	T	E	R	H	D	O	K
B	E	Y	D	V	O	H	Z	L	V	B	X	Y	N	F	N	L	Y
G	N	Q	L	I	L	B	E	N	A	V	O	N	A	L	A	T	N
R	G	X	C	S	M	K	T	A	D	I	J	F	G	Y	C	C	T
Q	B	E	N	M	A	C	D	U	I	L	M	Z	L	A	R	H	M	Q	V
S	H	Q	P	X	N	M	L	C	V	G	T	N	U	R	H	M	X	S	P
C	A	M	B	O	D	A	C	H	U	S	B	V	D	Y	L	O	U	T	Z
V	G	Z	F	O	M	N	R	X	L	Y	W	P	Q	P	G	R	M	W	R
Y	L	G	Q	P	K	C	A	I	R	N	G	O	R	M	J	K	L	B	S
T	N	H	I	J	Z	O	R	Y	A	W	L	V	N	H	T	R	S	P	V

Names are either down or across

Match up the eggs in pairs to complete the names of five birds.

ROW

CAN

FIN

CON

TURE

SPAR

PELI

PUF

FAL

VUL

What are the missing numbers on the post?

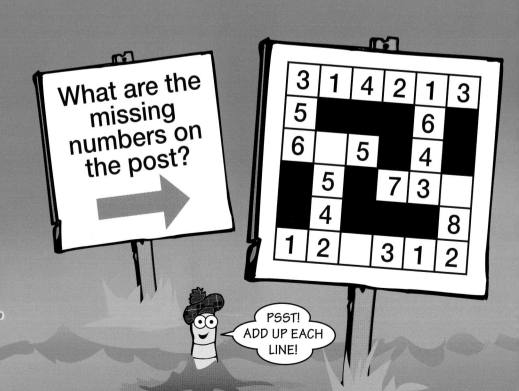

3	1	4	2	1	3
5					6
6		5		4	
	5		7	3	
	4				8
1	2		3	1	2

PSST! ADD UP EACH LINE!

0

THE DOG HOME

How many times can you find the words 'Corgi' and 'Poodle' in the kennel? The names can be down or across.

P	C	L	C	R	P	C	R	O	D	C
O	O	D	O	L	O	G	C	L	P	O
O	R	M	R	Y	O	F	O	M	O	R
C	G	T	G	S	D	N	R	O	O	G
R	I	L	I	O	L	E	G	L	D	I
C	O	R	G	I	E	R	I	P	L	C
D	C	P	O	O	D	L	E	O	E	T
N	O	V	P	Y	C	R	U	O	G	D
G	R	B	T			C	D	O	O	
M	G	S	Y			M	L	R	T	
D	I	Q	L			D	E	G	L	

$$5 + \square + 2 + \square + 1 = 18$$

CORGI   POODLE

LINK-UPS

Take the last letter of each animal's name and arrange them to spell the name of another animal.

MYSTIC GLEN

ere is a signpost at the bottom of the Glen, but what does
ay? The symbols on the signpost can be found scattered
oss the Glen - they will reveal the letters you need to
·ck the code.

You will find six creatures in the Glen.
Arrange the last letters from their
names to spell something you could
catch in a river in Scotland.

_ _ _ _ _ _

Which four of the
six creatures would
you NOT find in the
wild in Scotland?

ISLAND HOPPING

Scotland has just over 780 islands, here are just eleven of them. Can you place them in the grid?

COLONSAY

SANDAY

FOULA

BENBECULA

ARRAN

BUTE

IONA

WESTRAY

SKYE

MULL

COLL

The shortest scheduled flight in the world is between the islands of Westray and Papa Westray in the Orkneys. It takes only one minute, fourteen seconds to travel the one and a half miles between them!

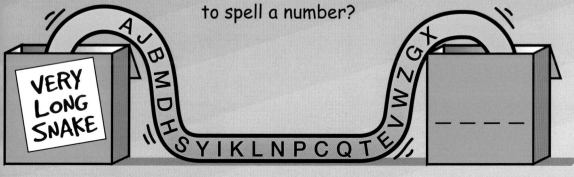

LOCH NESS

There are many Lochs in Scotland. One of the most famous is Loch Ness which is said to be the home of a large creature. No one has proved that the monster exists. but who knows? Place these eight lochs into the grid.

MONSTER

We have managed to take two photos of the Loch Ness Monster, but there seems to be eight differences between them. Do you see them?

QUICK QUIZ

Complete the eight words using these clues

1) They swim in water

2) He climbed a beanstalk

3) Falling ice particles

4) Looks like a butterfly

5) Not tame

6) Child's card game

7) Small particles on a beach

8) Opposite of narrow

1) _ _ S _

2) _ _ C _

3) _ _ O _

4) _ _ T _

5) _ _ L _

6) _ _ A _

7) _ _ N _

8) _ _ D _

POST WORDS

Place the four words below into the boxes on the post to spell two items of clothing

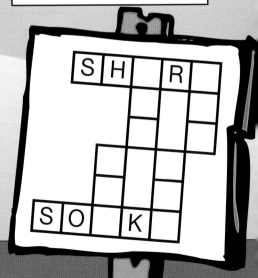

INK   TOP

BUS   ARC

'B' HIVES

How many of the word BEE can you find in Beehive 1 and can you find six four-letter words beginning with 'B' in Beehive 2?

C	L	M	B	E	B	V	N	T	U
B	E	E	O	D	E	M	B	E	E
H	B	K	L	B	E	O	R	B	C
E	E	B	C	E	Q	B	O	E	N
R	V	E	L	E	O	E	B	E	H
S	Y	E	T	B	R	E	I	V	B
N	B	E	E	N	B	E	E	B	E
K	D	C	B	E	E	H	U	L	E
Y	B	E	E	R	M	B	T	N	R

Words are either down or Across

B	A	V	B	V	R	B	C	Y	T
H	B	A	L	L	T	Q	R	B	L
U	L	B	P	W	Y	T	B	I	U
S	N	V	B	L	B	S	T	K	M
B	I	H	E	V	O	N	W	E	K
C	J	G	L	R	N	B	A	R	N
M	B	R	L	D	E	I	L	T	Z
B	O	O	T	E	G	L	J	P	Q
R	T	Y	R	M	L	S	B	O	V

Words are either down or Across

FRUIT

APPLE STALL

? ? ?

T O R

O W A

P N W

A D S P T E

Place three of the apples below on top of the three sets of apples on the left and change the three letter words to four letter words. The remaining three letters will spell the name of an animal.

___ ___ ___

STRAWBERRY STALL

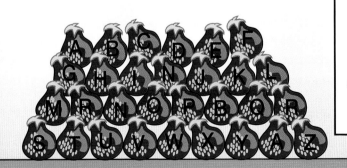

A B C D E F
G H I J K L
M N O P Q R
S T U V W X Y Z

There are thirty letters of the alphabet on the strawberries, with four letters of the alphabet having been duplicated. Find the extra four letters and arrange them to spell something you could find on a farm.

___ ___ ___ ___

STALLS

PEAR SEARCH

There are three pears missing from this stall. You will find them hidden somewhere amongst the other stalls. can you arrange the letters on them together with the two letters on the pears on the stall to spell the name of a country?

? ? ? **I** **N**

_ _ _ _ _

MELONS

Move one number from melon 'A' to melon 'B' so that the numbers on both melons have the same total.

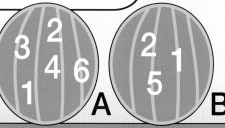

Melon A: 3 2 4 6 1
Melon B: 2 1 5

PINEAPPLE SEARCH

There should be five pineapples on this stall, which will spell the name of something you would find in school. Find the three missing pineapples to complete the word.

? **U** ? **E** ?

_ _ _ _ _

FOXY BOXES

I HAVE DRAWN A FOX ON EACH OF THESE SEVEN BOXES. WHICH TWO ARE EXACTLY THE SAME?

Transfer two of the letters from the word FOXY to the blue box and complete the four-letter word.

FOXY

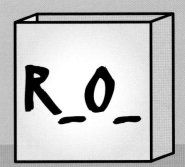

R_O_

SCOTS WORDS

Here is a list of twelve Scots words and their meanings. Try and find the Scots words in the grid below.

BAIRN	child
BUNNET	soft flat hat
DROOKIT	soaking wet
DUNT	knock against
TATTIE	potato
BRAW	fine
LOCH	lake
BRIG	bridge
GREET	weep
TREWS	tartan trousers
LASSIE	girl
KEN	know

YE AULD SCOTTISH WORDSEARCH

C	Y	D	J	S	K	L	P	V	R	G	Y	D	M
B	A	I	R	N	Q	A	D	R	F	N	T	Y	R
L	T	F	P	Y	V	S	B	G	B	R	A	W	G
N	K	Z	H	L	R	S	G	L	D	W	H	L	J
V	E	E	T	D	B	I	R	Y	T	F	G	H	V
R	N	M	R	V	L	E	E	S	A	I	J	L	P
D	G	P	E	O	B	L	E	N	T	G	B	M	Q
Q	W	L	W	N	R	W	T	V	T	Q	U	P	U
M	K	Y	S	Z	I	X	N	J	I	R	N	V	W
B	L	O	C	H	G	C	D	K	E	Z	N	Y	H
P	S	T	Q	J	N	D	U	N	T	U	E	V	B
V	D	R	O	O	K	I	T	P	B	W	T	N	Z
R	L	H	M	T	J	Y	C	V	L	K	F	L	T

The words are either Down or Across

NAME GAMES

Using the six clues, complete the words on the block and reveal the name of a type of vegetable.

1) BABY'S BED (3)
2) BACK OF YOUR FOOT (4)
3) SHOUTS OUT LOUD (5)
4) TALK (5)
5) BLACK BIRD (4)
6) JAPANESE MONEY (3)

NUMBER 6 BEGINS WITH "

TRANSFER THREE LETTERS FROM BOX 1 TO BOX 2 TO SPELL A BOY'S NAME!

N J I P H

_ O _ _

ALPHABET WINDOWS

1

A	J	C	D	P	F	G	T
Z							I
L							B
X							K
R							Y
V	U	H	S	Q	E	N	M

1 _ _ _

2

A	V	C	D	F	G	H	I
Z							J
K							Y
X							L
W							M
B	U	N	S	Q	P	O	T

2 _ _ _ _

3

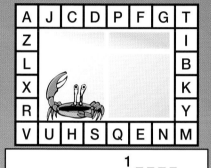

B	V	D	L	F	Q	H	I
Z							J
Y							K
X							E
W							M
C	U	T	R	G	P	O	N

3 _ _ _

4

B	T	D	E	Y	G	H	I
Z							J
L							K
X							O
V							M
U	C	S	R	Q	P	F	N

4 _ _ _ _

TAKE THE FIRST TWO LETTERS OF THE ANIMAL IN THE WINDOW, PLUS THE TWO LETTERS MISSING FROM THE ALPHABET, TO MAKE THE NAME OF ANOTHER CREATURE

HOWL OR GROWL

Can you match each animal to the sound it makes?

FROG   HOOTS

DONKEY   ROARS

ELEPHANT   BRAYS

LION   CROAKS

WOLF   QUACKS

MONKEY   TRUMPETS

OWL   GIBBERS

DUCK   HOWLS

WHICH ONE IS THE ODD ONE OUT?

LION	WOLF
CHEETAH	TIGER

I WONDER WHAT SOU
A WORM MAKES...
...GROWL?

CREEPY CASTLE

CAN YOU SPOT THE EIGHT DIFFERENCES BETWEEN THESE TWO PHOTOS?

COME ON JIG. LET'S SEE WHAT'S IN THE CELLAR!

THE CREEPY

FLOCK

QUIZ SEARCH
The answers to these six questions are hidden in the cellar. Can you find them?

1) What is the capital of Austria?
   _____

2) What animal lives in a Sett?
   _____

3) What was invented first, the bicycle or the Bus?
   _____

4) Which planet is the largest, Jupiter or Mars?
   _____

5) Which country has the largest population in the world?
   _____

6) What do you call a group of Camels?
   _____

ONLY ONE OF THE FOUR DOORS IN THE CELLAR WILL LEAD YOU OUT, THE OTHER THREE ARE FALSE DOORS. REARRANGE THE LETTERS ON EACH DOOR TO SPELL SOMETHING YOU CAN EAT. THE ODD ONE OUT OF THE FOUR IS THE REAL WAY OUT. GOOD LUCK... HA...HA...HA...HA!

SPOOKY DOWN HERE, ISN'T IT?

WHERE DID YOU COME FROM?

WAY OUT

1
TAPOOT

CLUE, Begins with a 'p'

_ _ _ _ _ _

WAY OUT

2
TRACOR

CLUE, Begins with a 'c'

_ _ _ _ _ _

BADGER

CASTLE CELLAR

Each line of this verse is a clue to a letter which will spell a five-letter word.

MY FIRST IS IN CAR, BUT NOT IN TRAM.

MY SECOND IS IN RAM, BUT NOT IN LAMB.

MY THIRD IS IN ONE, BUT NOT IN NINE.

MY FOURTH IS IN WATER AND ALSO IN WINE.

MY LAST IS IN SINGLE AND ALSO IN STACK.

MY WHOLE ARE CREATURES WHICH ARE COMPLETELY BLACK

BEFORE YOU LEAVE THE CELLAR, CAN YOU SOLVE MY RIDDLE?

CHINA

BOX BOGGLER

Find the three missing letters of the alphabet, then use the letters to spell an animal.

S	J	Y	B	G
D	V	P	L	U
N	A	Z	T	E
H	K	R	C	M
W		Q		I

BICYCLE

WAY OUT

3 PAGER

CLUE: Begins with a 'G'

_ _ _ _ _

SEE YOU LATER!

OH NO YOU WONT!

WAY OUT

4 PINRUT

CLUE: Begins with a 'T'

_ _ _ _ _ _

VIENNA

CASTLE SNAPS

This castle has been photographed eight times, but only two of them are exactly the same. Which two?

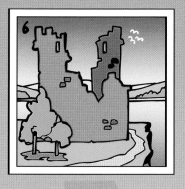

WILDLIFE SEARCH

Here are eight endangered species of wildlife which can be found in and around Scotland. Can you find them in the grid? The names can be either down or across.

OSPREY · BADGER · CAPERCAILLIE
OTTER · BASKING SHARK
SEAL · PINE MARTEN · WILDCAT

F	L	T	B	R	U	V	Q	S	W	F	C	I	V
L	C	N	W	Q	M	C	D	N	I	U	Z	B	P
N	A	R	O	S	P	R	E	Y	L	P	Q	A	R
Z	P	K	Z	B	S	X	L	X	D	I	J	S	F
T	E	P	L	N	E	M	S	P	C	N	M	K	N
U	R	D	M	T	A	Y	J	Q	A	E	P	I	W
P	C	L	I	O	L	R	M	V	T	M	S	N	T
V	A	B	A	D	G	E	R	Y	L	A	F	G	Y
R	I	Y	T	V	P	J	O	V	Y	R	P	S	K
K	L	G	U	D	Y	N	Z	M	K	T	U	H	N
J	L	N	E	O	T	T	E	R	P	E	S	A	T
M	I	H	Y	R	Q	L	T	S	X	N	L	R	Y
Y	E	T	C	X	M	V	W	N	T	M	C	K	B
X	V	U	N	T	B	P	C	F	N	I	N	T	Z

The Capercaillie is a large woodland grouse found in the pinewood forests of Scotland. Their population has declined rapidly and there are now fewer than 1,000 compared to the 20,000 in the 1970's.

A MAZE N' BRIDGES

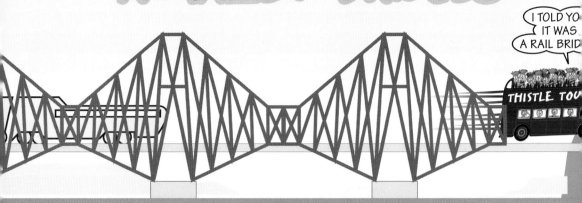

The Forth Rail Bridge is one of the of the most famous bridges in the world. Stretching for 1.5 miles across the River Forth it took eight years to build and 55,000 tons of steel was used in its construction. It was completed in 1890.

Here are the four main types of Bridge.

BEAM   **SUSPENSION**   **ARCH**   **CANTILEVER**

Can you complete the maze by only going over or under arch or cantilever bridges?

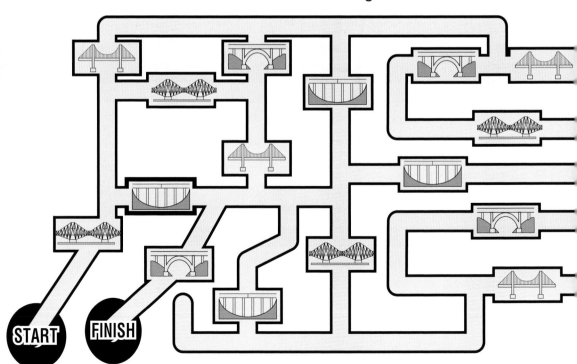

QUIZ SEARCH

Answer each of the four questions and remove the letters of each answer from the grid. The four remaining letters will spell a 4-letter word.

1) What is the capital of Norway?
A) PARIS
B) TOKYO
C) OSLO

2) Which creature has no eyes?
A) SPIDER
B) WORM
C) SHARK

3) What do you call a strong wind?
A) BREEZE
B) GALE
C) FLUTTER

4) Which is the closest to Earth?
A) MOON
B) SUN
C) MARS

Grid letters:
B O
E T
O W O M N L
L O I S E O
R M
A G

Arrange the letters of these three words to spell three other words.

1) PART   2) BLOW   3) TRAMS

_ _ _ _   _ _ _ _   _ _ _ _ _

The Highland Games are held in various parts of Scotland every year.
The Games consist of many events which include Tossing the Caber, Putting the Stone,
Throwing the Hammer, Tug of War, Highland Dancing and Pipers.

THISTLES
TUG OF WAR

This contest isn't fair. There are more Thistles
on the West Side than there are on the East.
So which number on the West Side should you
move to the East Side, so that both sets of
numbers add up to the same total?

OI!

9   4   3   6   12   5   8   2   13   4

WEST
SIDE

CLUE:
Work out the difference,
and divide by 2

EAST
SIDE

34

A RIDDLE FROM JIG

Each line of each verse is a clue to two 5-letter words.
Can you solve the riddles?

MY FIRST IS IN THREE, BUT NOT IN THIRD. ☐
MY SECOND IS IN TWIRL, BUT NOT IN STIRRED. ☐
MY THIRD IS IN PAGE, BUT NOT IN PAPER. ☐
MY FOURTH IS IN STRIP, BUT NOT IN SCRAPER. ☐
MY LAST IS IN SMILING AND ALSO IN FROWN. ☐
MY WHOLE IS A NORTHERN SCOTTISH TOWN.

A RIDDLE FROM JAG

MY FIRST IS IN WOOL, BUT NOT IN WOOD. ☐
MY SECOND IS IN DOOR, BUT NOT IN RUDE. ☐
MY THIRD IS IN COAT, BUT NOT IN BOAT. ☐
MY FOURTH IS IN HAT, BUT NOT IN GOAT. ☐
MY LAST IS IN STIR AND ALSO IN SHAKES. ☐
MY WHOLE IS THE SCOTTISH WORD FOR LAKES.

BOGGLERS

BOX BOGGLER
Find the three missing letters of the alphabet from the grid, then make a 3-letter word from them.

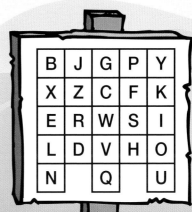

B	J	G	P	Y
X	Z	C	F	K
E	R	W	S	I
L	D	V	H	O
N		Q		U

1 TO 5
Only one letter of the alphabet can complete all five words on the sign post. What are the words?

WORM MARATHON
START

I'M TAKING PART IN THE MARATHON. THEN I'M HEADING FOR THE RED ZONE!

RIVER TRAIL

Find the ten rivers in the grid

The River Tay is the longest river in Scotland, covering a distance of 188km (117m)

Names are either Down or Across

DEVERON

TWEED

TAY

SPEY

C	P	T	A	Y	B	W	R	L	Y	P	V
R	Q	N	P	J	L	F	S	D	O	N	C
D	E	E	V	C	M	H	P	T	D	K	X
T	F	Z	W	L	N	S	E	N	E	R	M
L	O	K	H	Y	I	J	Y	L	V	S	F
Y	R	S	G	D	C	D	F	X	E	M	J
S	T	F	N	E	F	K	G	B	R	V	B
K	H	D	T	W	E	E	D	Z	O	H	Q
L	Y	R	P	B	G	M	K	S	N	Y	P
F	I	N	D	H	O	R	N	B	Z	K	F
V	J	C	K	Q	A	N	N	A	N	D	L
G	L	F	Y	H	N	J	L	X	K	S	G

FINDHORN

DEE

I THINK IT HAS CAUGHT YOU!

HA HA

I'VE CAUGHT A SALMON

CLYDE

ANNAN

DON

FORTH

NO FISHING

CREATURE QUIZ

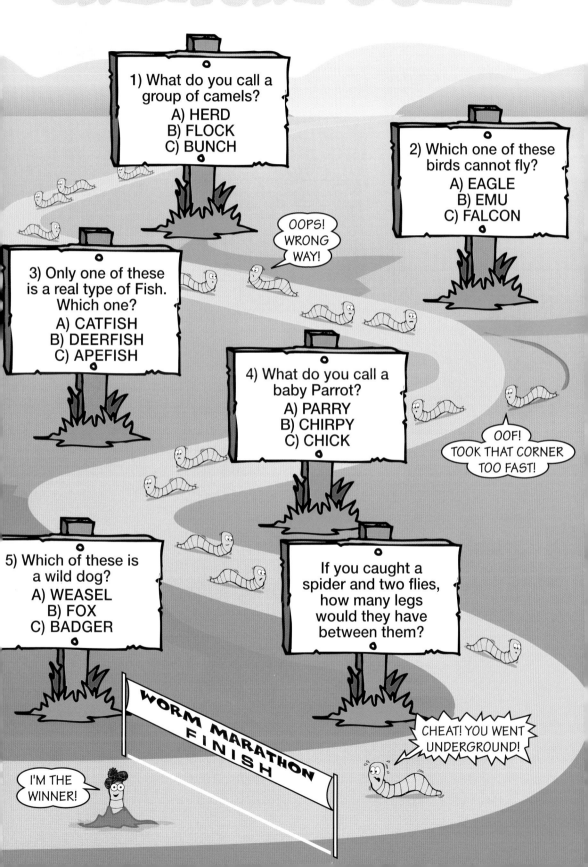

PLAY THE

Using the eight clues, can you complete the eight words which all begin with a letter from the word BAGPIPES?

1) Creature that builds dams   B _ _ _ _ _

2) A Continent   A _ _ _ _ _ _

3) A place to grow flowers   G _ _ _ _ _

4) Talking Bird   P _ _ _ _ _

5) Eskimo Shelters   I _ _ _ _ _

6) Large Snake   P _ _ _ _ _

7) Tower in Paris   E _ _ _ _ _

8) A Planet   S _ _ _ _ _

WHAT INSTRUMENT DO SHEEP LIKE TO PLAY? THE BAAAGPIPES!

BAGPIPES

Here are eight photos of Jag playing the Bagpipes, each of them has a letter of the alphabet. Only four of the photos are identical, Can you find them and arrange the letters to spell a four letter word that has something to do with Bagpipes?

_ _ _ _

TONGUE TWISTER
How fast can you say this?
BONNIE BELLA BROWN BLEW BAGPIPES
AT THE BONNYBRIDGE BAGPIPE FAIR

HIGHLAND FLING

The Highland fling is the oldest of the traditional Scottish dances. It is a solo dance originally performed on a shield called a Targe and is danced on one spot.
Here are eight photos of Jig doing the Highland fling, but only two of them are the same. Which two?

WARNING
Very few make it through the RED ZONE. Can you? →

WARNING
Once you enter you can't turn back! →

IF YOU DON'T MIND, WE'LL JUST STOP HERE FOR A REST!

GOOD LUCK!

WARNING
Even Jig and Jag are avoiding the RED ZONE. Are you up to the challenge? →

THAT RED ZONE IS TOO HOT FOR ME!

FIND THE BIRD

Hidden in the grid below is the name of a Bird of Prey that can be found in Scotland. Place the sixteen words into the grid to reveal it!

WIG • FLOUR • CLIMB • EVENT • FERRY
TENT • BUS • YEARNING • OUR • EARN • CAVE
LION • FIFTY • COLLECT • PRIDE • ONCE

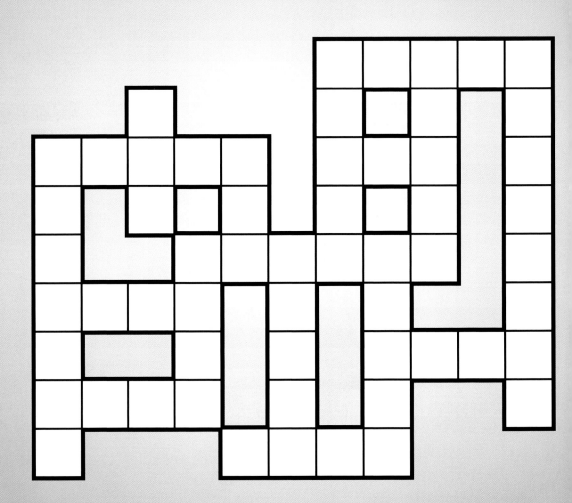

Which of these four birds can fly backwards?

PELICAN • HUMMINGBIRD • CROW • EAGLE

CLUSTERS

Only four of the five groups of letters can fit into the box. Can you place the correct group into each corner?

A
PLAY
TEA
HUT
SHOP

B
MOLE TWO
TAR TRUE

C
NEWS
ONE
OUT
FREE

E
CAVE
VET
ANT
COAT

D
WING
YEN
HAY
SHOW

(grid with numbers 1, 2, 3, 4 and letter Y)

OOPS... SOMEONE HAS LEFT A LETTER IN THE GRID!

WORDS OUT

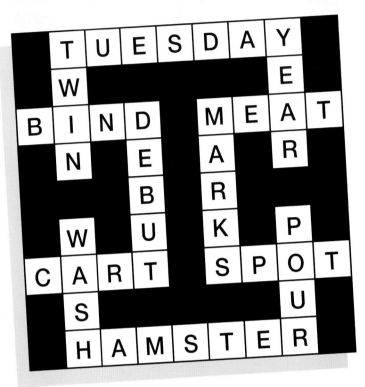

HOW MANY 3-LETTER WORDS CAN YOU FIND IN THIS CROSSWORD?

HOW MANY OF THE WORD 'THISTLE' CAN YOU FIND IN THIS GRID?

H	S	L	T	H	I	S	T	L	E	T	P
T	H	I	S	T	L	E	L	E	S	H	O
P	V	T	L	O	U	V	E	P	T	I	Q
L	T	H	S	U	R	M	S	L	E	S	R
E	H	I	T	H	I	S	T	L	E	T	L
R	I	S	L	T	P	L	V	S	L	L	T
M	S	T	E	H	L	T	T	E	P	E	S
O	T	L	N	I	T	H	I	S	T	L	E
U	L	E	V	S	R	D	P	V	R	U	O
Z	E	O	C	T	T	H	I	S	T	L	E
P	V	L	D	L	R	L	Q	S	L	E	S
Q	U	T	P	E	K	P	R	N	D	R	M

The words can be either Down or Across

Zoo VIEW

FRY

ELM

INK

EVE

SPY

WIG

ADD

PEG

SKY

ONE

ODD

USE

ELF

HOT

OWN

ASK

OLD

DIG

SHY

FOG

Place the 3-letter words on the roofs into the zoo complex to reveal the names of sixteen creatures.

S E A   O R M
S N A L   M O U S E
O B S T E   S T R
B S W A   E E R I C
T E
U L   E
L T O A   L U G U
U R   I
T   R
G   B
G E R O O   I O N

THE AULD SCOTTISH

SOOR PLOOMS | **PENNY DAINTIES** | **SHERBERT LEMONS** | **BUTTERSCOTCH** | **MINT HUMBUGS** | **GOB STOPPERS** | **TABLET**

9 CARAMELS	**11** ECLAIRS	**16** TOFFEES	**14** ECLAIRS	**7** CARAMELS

NOTE PAD

12 ECLAIRS	**31** TOFFEES	**18** ECLAIRS	**14** CARAMELS	**24** TOFFEES

9 TOFFEES	**13** CARAMELS	**16** ECLAIRS	**14** TOFFEES	**10** CARAMEL

12 TOFFEES

JAR SWITCH

There are fifteen jars of Eclairs, Toffees and Caramels. Jig wants to put twice as many Toffees as there are Eclairs or Caramels on the shelves. So which jar should Jig replace with the jar of twelve Toffees?

Free the Horses

There are thirty horses trapped in the centre of the grids. To free them you must find the names of 30 creatures hidden in the grids. Cross out a horse for each creature you find. The names are either down or across.

```
S F B R C A T L Y P O B M R C O W V
N R F I E D M Q P I H E G N Q G X L
P O L G T R C R C G Y E S Q P O L I
V G S L I J V N Q M L T N L X Y A Z
X K F V G T P Y B E A R O I Z T B A
M O U K E L U R T Q S D U O H L Y R
C M T Y R O C T O P U S V N B Q Z D
H W                               E R
I J     C R O W J N T C N X T M   B T
C Q     B U T T E R F L Y S O R   R U
K X     M W                 A Y   A V
E W           [horses]       D C   P A
N W     R N   [horses]       Q T   N L
X T     S P   [horses]       J B   Z L
K U     H Q   [horses]       H K   T I
J R     E J   [horses]       R V   O G
V T     E N                 C E   U A
H L     P C H L H T G O A T N E   M T
Q E     M D O G M B X W V P U L   K O
                                   G R

S J S P M T H N Q W S H A R K U I H
N Y D Q O E L E P H A N T S Z L R J
A M E Y N L M R B Y K P W T U Q A W
K N E B K H B L J Q V O N N J K F Y
E W R C E T V R I Z S P I D E R F P
B Z Q D Y J N A O W V B R T H U E T
R C L V P U X T N D F L V A P E C X
```

HOME COMFORTS

Place these seven items into the grid below. The other three items missing from the grid can be found somewhere on this page. Can you name them?

RADIO

COMPUTER

PHONE

SEAT

CARPET

LAMP

ORNAMENTS

GREAT
SCOTS
PART 1

BLOCKHEADS

Each block should consist of four words, two across and two down. Using only letters which are in the centre of each block, can you complete the words? The same letter can be used more than once in the same word.

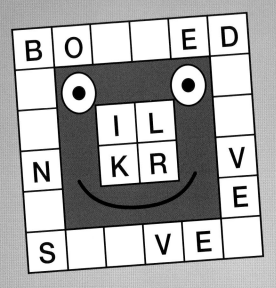

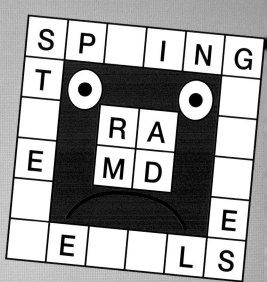

BOGGLE SQUARES

Place the four, 3-letter words into each square and complete four 6-letter words.

1

```
      D O W
      O   I
      G
E
T A   T E S
```

2

```
        N E R
        E   E
        W
D
S P   A K S
```

BUS • PER • WIN • ALL   LAY • RAN • EWE • BAN

TOWN TOURS

Can you find the fourteen Scottish towns on the signpost in the grid?

B	A	L	G	F	T	C	E	L	D	N	F	M	H	J
P	R	O	H	V	J	H	S	L	F	O	R	F	A	R
F	B	N	B	K	Z	A	B	K	G	M	P	G	C	S
C	R	G	W	A	F	M	X	H	Y	I	W	B	V	D
V	O	Z	M	Y	N	I	L	D	F	S	N	J	F	M
J	A	N	O	H	Q	L	G	R	E	E	N	O	C	K
M	T	L	N	C	K	T	Q	B	D	P	R	F	G	J
K	H	A	T	F	S	O	A	L	L	O	A	A	L	B
L	P	N	R	M	N	N	T	G	Z	M	J	L	F	R
B	H	A	O	K	I	R	Q	A	E	D	Y	K	H	E
F	J	R	S	G	V	C	J	W	D	T	L	I	K	C
D	S	K	E	P	B	W	F	N	V	H	N	R	D	H
S	T	R	A	N	R	A	E	R	M	Q	B	K	L	I
L	M	K	S	K	I	L	M	A	R	N	O	C	K	N
C	G	F	K	I	R	K	C	A	L	D	Y	L	G	C

OBAN ELGIN

BRECHIN
ARBROATH
FORFAR
MONTROSE

KIRKCALDY
FALKIRK
ALLOA

GREENOCK
KILMARNOCK
STRANRAER

HAMILTON
LANARK

The names can be Down, Across or Diagonal

I SAY WE TAKE THE HIGH ROAD!

I SAY THE LOW ROAD!

THE HIGH ROAD!

THE LOW ROAD!

WILL YOU MAKE YOUR MIND UP!

THISTLE TOURS

RED HOT RIDDLES

Each line of this verse is a clue to a letter which will spell the name of a place in Scotland.

MY FIRST IS IN REAL, BUT NOT IN TRUE. ☐
MY SECOND IS IN RED, BUT NOT IN BLUE. ☐
MY THIRD IS IN EAR, BUT NOT IN HEAD. ☐
MY FOURTH IS IN LEADER, BUT NOT IN LED. ☐
MY LAST IS IN PEN AND ALSO IN NOTE. ☐
MY WHOLE CAN BE REACHED BY USING A BOAT.

This verse will spell the name of a famous Scot.

MY FIRST IS IN BOAT, BUT NOT IN FLOAT. ☐
MY SECOND IS IN SKUNK, BUT NOT IN STOAT. ☐
MY THIRD IS IN GREEN, BUT NOT IN BLUE. ☐
MY FOURTH IS IN MINCE, BUT NOT IN STEW. ☐
MY LAST IS IN HASTE AND ALSO IN SLOW. ☐
MY WHOLE IS A PERSON WHO LIVED LONG AGO.

FACT OR FICTION

Which of the ten statements
below are true and which ones are false?

1 Penguins live
at the North Pole.

TRUE ☐ FALSE ☐

2 A Gondola is
a large fish.

TRUE ☐ FALSE ☐

3 Gorillas
build nests.

TRUE ☐ FALSE ☐

4 Florida is the
largest state in
the USA.

TRUE ☐ FALSE ☐

5 A fedora
is a type of hat.

TRUE ☐ FALSE ☐

6 Sound travels faster
through water than it
does through air.

TRUE ☐ FALSE ☐

7 Camels store fat
in their humps.

TRUE ☐ FALSE ☐

8 A Marlin is a
type of vegetable.

TRUE ☐ FALSE ☐

9 Mars has
two moons.

TRUE ☐ FALSE ☐

10 An octagon
has six sides.

TRUE ☐ FALSE ☐

Castles

BLAIR   TULLIBOLE   BALFOUR   ABERDOUR

OMLONGON   AROS   DUNVEGAN   LEWS

ARCALDINE   CULZEAN   GLAMIS   KELBURN

THESE TWELVE CASTLES ARE HIDDEN IN THE GRID. CAN YOU FIND THEM?

V	A	W	Y	P	Q	A	L	N	B	H	B	D
P	B	H	L	S	N	P	R	Z	V	T	L	S
U	E	J	R	E	G	D	Y	O	L	U	A	B
Z	R	L	B	Y	W	L	H	J	S	Q	I	A
G	D	M	A	R	M	S	P	M	R	W	R	L
L	O	K	R	V	C	U	L	Z	E	A	N	F
A	U	E	C	N	B	H	K	W	B	L	M	O
M	R	L	A	D	U	N	V	E	G	A	N	U
I	W	B	L	T	Z	G	C	D	H	V	O	R
S	K	U	D	C	O	M	L	O	N	G	O	N
L	P	R	I	W	N	J	H	Z	T	Y	P	Q
J	T	N	N	T	U	L	L	I	B	O	L	E
U	V	H	E	P	D	N	L	B	V	U	Z	J

JAG'S CASTLE

FACT,
Balmoral Castle was built by Queen Victoria. It is the Scottish home of the Royal Family.

THE NAMES CAN BE DOWN, ACROSS OR DIAGONAL

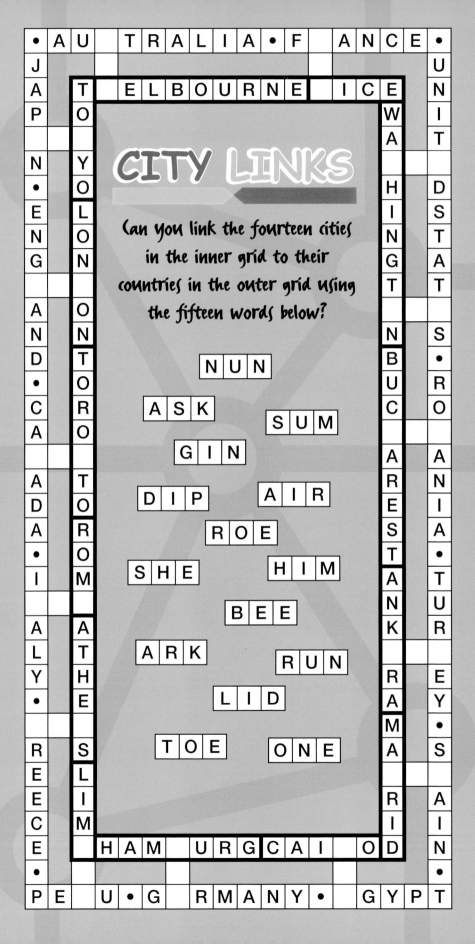

CITY LINKS

Can you link the fourteen cities in the inner grid to their countries in the outer grid using the fifteen words below?

NUN

ASK   SUM

GIN

DIP   AIR

ROE

SHE   HIM

BEE

ARK   RUN

LID

TOE   ONE

TRIPLE SNAP

There are twelve cards below, each with two letters. Find four sets of three matching cards and arrange each group of six letters to spell four words.

B

L

C

K

L

O

D

O

P

E

C

U

B

E

D

S

W

T

A

N

W

B

U

1) _ _ _ _ _ _   2) _ _ _ _ _ _

3) _ _ _ _ _ _   4) _ _ _ _ _ _

BATS

Complete the fourteen words on the grid using only the letters from the word BATS.

The BAT Wall

There are fourteen bats each with a number on it, hanging from the wall below. Can you work out what numbers should be on the three bats in the middle?

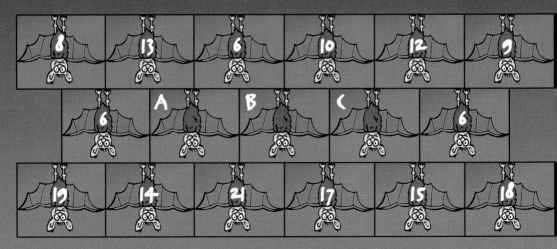

CLUELESS CROSSWORDS

MAKE A MEAL

Here are six types of Scottish food.

PORRIDGE • HAGGIS • OATCAKES • STOVIES • SCONES • SHORTBREAD

Can you place them onto the dish together with these twelve other types of food and ingredients?

SUGAR • VEAL • RICE • LEMON • NUTMEG • SAUCE • TOMATOES • EGG
MINT • COCONUT • COD • POTATOES

START WITH THE SHORTBREAD

SHORTBREAD

10 from 11

B	P	U	D	L	V
A	Z	C	T	I	E
O	S	V	B	K	R
U	T	R	O	A	G
N	Y	N	D	P	F
•	L	U	M	E	R

R	L	M	D	S	J
B	X	F	N	K	N
K	V	K	T	Y	H
Y	A	C	E	N	C
S	P	Z	L	R	W
P	G	Q	N	O	•

10 from 11
10 from 11
10 from 11

Only 10 of these 11 words are required to complete the alphabet. Which word is not needed?

_ _ _

Bubbles: STY, ACE, DOT, CAR, SKY, VET, AGE, TIE, INK, AXE, APE

Left side letters: A, B, D, F, H, J, L, M

Right side letters: N, O, Q, S, U, W, Y, Z

Only 10 of the same 11 words can be found in the four grids. Which word is missing?

_ _ _

•	M	I	P	X	W
H	O	N	Y	B	G
N	X	K	C	L	T
V	E	T	N	J	D
R	U	P	A	G	E
B	V	L	C	T	R

Y	B	C	D	G	•
S	A	L	O	P	H
W	X	N	T	V	C
U	E	D	K	O	J
N	T	O	L	F	I
R	M	Q	B	U	L

10 from 11
10 from 11
10 from 11

THE MONSTER

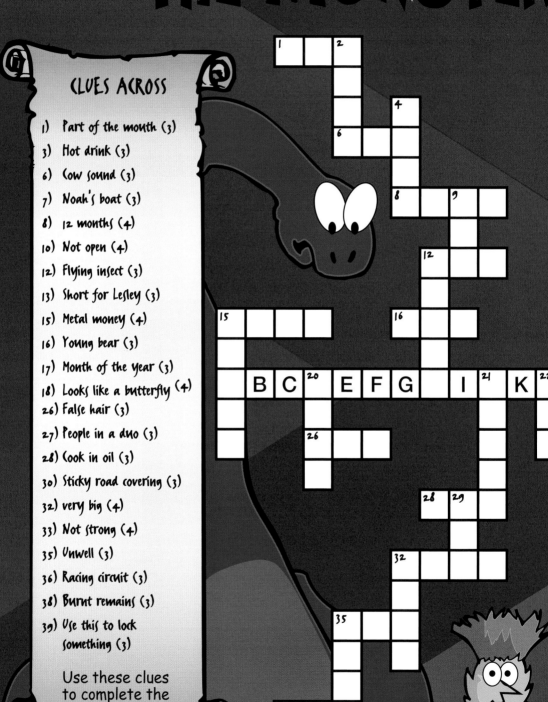

CLUES ACROSS

1) Part of the mouth (3)
3) Hot drink (3)
6) Cow sound (3)
7) Noah's boat (3)
8) 12 months (4)
10) Not open (4)
12) Flying insect (3)
13) Short for Lesley (3)
15) Metal money (4)
16) Young bear (3)
17) Month of the year (3)
18) Looks like a butterfly (4)
26) False hair (3)
27) People in a duo (3)
28) Cook in oil (3)
30) Sticky road covering (3)
32) very big (4)
33) Not strong (4)
35) Unwell (3)
36) Racing circuit (3)
38) Burnt remains (3)
39) Use this to lock something (3)

Use these clues to complete the alphabet!

18 ACROSS IS MOTH!

CROSSWORD

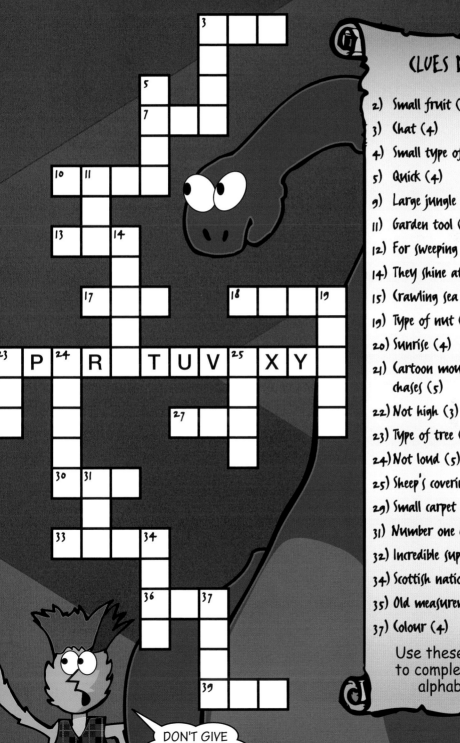

CLUES DOWN

2) Small fruit (4)

3) Chat (4)

4) Small type of horse (4)

5) Quick (4)

9) Large jungle creature (3)

11) Garden tool (3)

12) For sweeping the floor (5)

14) They shine at night (5)

15) Crawling sea creatures (5)

19) Type of nut (5)

20) Sunrise (4)

21) Cartoon mouse that Tom chases (5)

22) Not high (3)

23) Type of tree (3)

24) Not loud (5)

25) Sheep's covering (4)

29) Small carpet (3)

31) Number one card (3)

32) Incredible super hero (4)

34) Scottish national dress (4)

35) Old measurement (4)

37) Colour (4)

Use these clues to complete the alphabet!

THE WAILING WHALE

There is a whale trapped in the centre of the grid. Can you release it to join the other whale? To do so you have to place the seven groups of letters below into the grid to spell two 6-letter words and two 4-letter words.

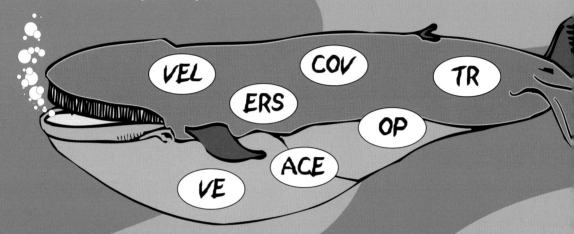

VEL · COV · TR · ERS · OP · ACE · VE

The Blue Whale is the largest mammal in the world.

W	H	A	L	E	W	H	A	L	E
W									W
H									H
A									A
L									L
E									E
S									S
W	H	A	L		W	H	A	L	E

Out of this World

There are twelve planets circling this Sun. Two of them are exactly the same. Which two?

Using the letter 'B' on the sun and a pair of letters, make nine 3-letter words. the remaining six letters will spell a word. What is it?

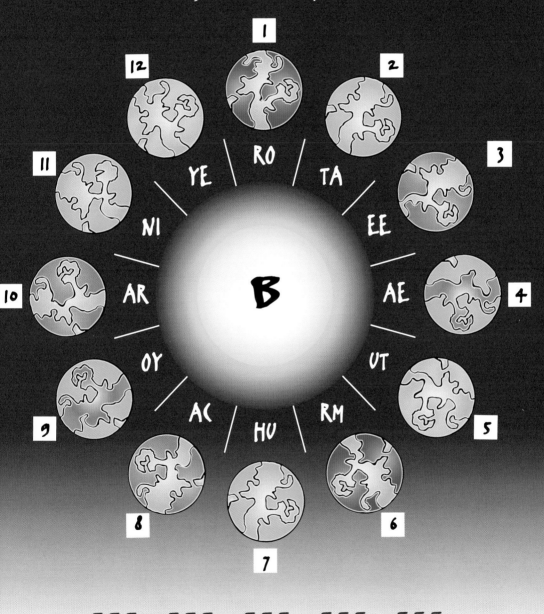

Six letter word _ _ _ _ _ _

GLOBE GRID

There are over 6,400,000,000 people in the world.

Place these 26 names into the grid above.

MOROCCO • HAITI • BERMUDA • AUSTRIA • CYPRUS • PORTUGAL
• CANADA • FIJI • MALAWI • ICELAND • PANAMA • MALI • FINLAND
• PARAGUAY • URUGUAY • OMAN • ITALY • ROMANIA • AUSTRALIA • SYR
• GUATEMALA • JAPAN • CHAD • INDIA • ZIMBABWE • NIGER

FLAG WAVING

The Scottish National flag is the Saltire which is derived from the St Andrew's Cross. The Lion Rampant flag is the Royal Coat of Arms adopted during the reign of King William 1, 'The Lion', who lived from 1143 to 1214.

Here are ten other national flags. Can you match each one to its country?

GREECE • ARGENTINA
USA • SPAIN • ITALY
FRANCE • RUSSIA
PORTUGAL • DENMARK
GERMANY

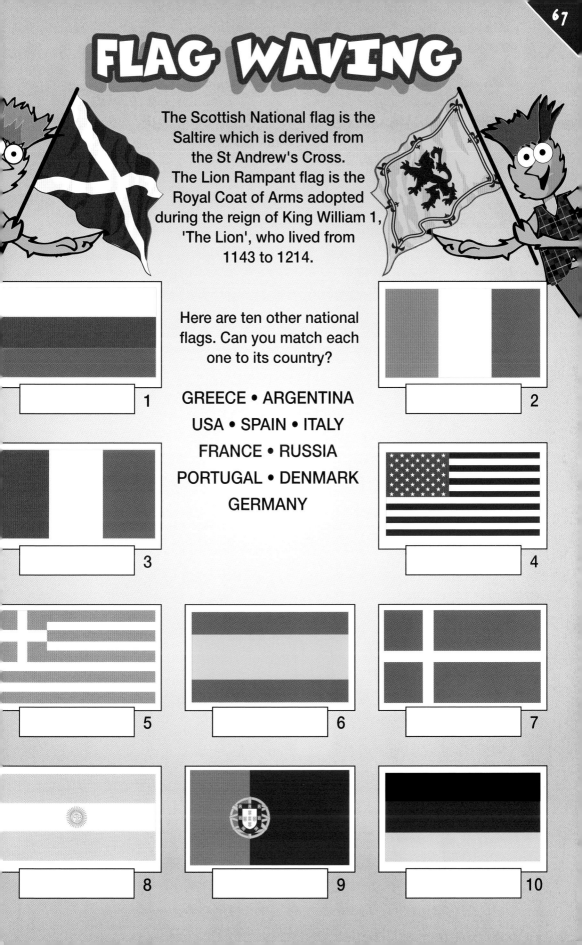

1

2

3

4

5

6

7

8

9

10

FAMOUS SCOTS

Andrew CARNEGIE
Built railway and steel companies then gave his wealth away.

Sir Alexander FLEMING
Discovered Penicillin.

David LIVINGSTONE
African explorer and Missionary.

Alexander Graham BELL
Inventor of the telephone.

Robert BURNS
World famous poet.

James WATT
Developed the steam engine.

Sir Walter SCOTT
Famous author.

Allan PINKERTON
Founded a detective agency in Chicago, USA.

David DALE
Created the largest cot spinning mills in Britain

Charles MACINTOSH
Invented waterproof clothing.

Here are eighteen famous Scots. Can you place ten of their surnames (which are in BOLD CAPITAL letters) into the grid and find the other eight surnames in the wordsearch

John Logie BAIRD
Television inventor.

William PATERSON
Founder of the Bank of England.

Sir James DEWAR
Vacuum flask inventor.

Alistair MACLEAN
Author.

Thomas TELFORD
Civil Engineer.

John BUCHAN
Author.

Sir J.M. BARRIE
Author of Peter Pan.

Sir Harry LAUDER
Entertainer.

C	S	J	Y	P	L	M	C	V	W	T	Q	M	R
N	O	S	B	G	Y	B	A	R	R	I	E	P	S
V	H	O	U	Q	H	K	L	S	G	V	Y	N	C
P	Q	R	C	B	I	J	T	A	S	H	V	F	B
T	G	K	H	Y	A	P	J	N	U	Z	P	Q	L
D	E	Z	A	G	M	I	P	W	D	D	Z	E	N
H	T	L	N	R	L	Q	R	K	E	M	E	P	Q
F	L	U	F	A	J	H	Z	D	W	A	T	R	O
J	N	O	S	O	T	M	R	Y	A	C	H	L	V
W	Y	V	P	M	R	B	Q	T	R	L	M	R	W
P	H	B	Q	C	Z	D	F	G	J	E	P	M	C
K	P	A	T	E	R	S	O	N	H	A	Q	K	J
M	B	L	P	Q	U	V	W	Z	Y	N	S	O	M
G	V	J	T	H	S	K	R	G	N	T	P	V	R

The names can be Down, Across or Diagonal.

THE SCOTTISH PUZZLE BOOK

BLUE ZONE

4) Password - KARTS.

7) Spot the difference 1) UP SIGN
2) GOAT'S HORN 3) BALLOON
4) BIRDS 5) CHICK IN NEST
6) ICE AXE 7) MOUNTAIN 8) FIELD.

8) Scrambled Eggs FALCON, PUFFIN,
SPARROW, VULTURE, PELICAN.
Missing numbers - 3, 4 AND 5.
ALL LINES TOTAL 14.

9) Dog Kennel - 6 CORGI, 4 POODLE.
Link-Ups - BEAR.

10) Signpost - THE CAPITAL OF
SCOTLAND IS EDINBURGH.

11) Six creatures - OCTOPUS, PANDA,
OWL, WORM, KANGAROO, PENGUIN
= SALMON. YOU WOULD NOT FIND A
PANDA, PENGUIN, KANGAROO OR
OCTOPUS IN SCOTLAND.

13) Jag in the Box - TOWN, MILK, BLUE,
SNAP, SALT, TENT. Snake - FOUR.

15) Spot the difference 1) CLOUDS
2) BIRDS 3) JAG 4) WOOD IN
MONSTER'S MOUTH 5) BRANCH ON
TREE 6) ROCK ON ISLAND
7) MONSTER'S FLIPPER
8) SHOAL OF FISH.

16) Quick Quiz - 1) FISH 2) JACK
3) SNOW 4) MOTH 5) WILD 6) SNAP
7) SAND 8) WIDE.
Post Words - SHIRT, SOCKS.

17) Beehive 1 - 12 BEE. Beehive 2 - BALL,
BIKE, BELL, BARN, BOOT, BONE.

18) Apple Stall - STOP, TOWN, DRAW.
Animal - APE. Strawberry Stall - BARN.

19) Pear Search - SPAIN.
Melons - MOVE NUMBER 4 SO BOTH
SETS OF NUMBERS TOTAL 12.
Pineapple Search - RULER.

20) Foxy Boxes - Foxes 2 & 7 are the same.
Four letter word ROOF.

22) Name Games - 1) COT 2) HEEL
3) MELON 4) SPEAK 5) CROW 6) YEN.
Boy's Name - JOHN.
Missing vegetable - CELERY.

23) Alphabet Windows 1) CROW 2) BEAR
3) SEAL 4) SWAN.

24) Howl or Growl FROG - CROAKS,
DONKEY - BRAYS,
ELEPHANT - TRUMPETS,
LION - ROARS, WOLF - HOWLS,
MONKEY - GIBBERS, OWL - HOOTS,
DUCK - QUACKS.
Odd One Out - WOLF, IT'S A WILD
DOG, THE OTHERS ARE WILD CATS.

25) Creepy Castle, Spot the difference
1) BOOKS 2) SPEAR 3) PICTURE ON
WALL 4) DESK LIGHT SWITCH
5) BUTTONS ON CHAIR
6) LEG OF CHAIR 7) DOOR HANDLE
8) DOOR PANEL.

26 & 27) Quiz Search - 1) VIENNA
2) BADGER 3) BICYCLE 4) JUPITER
5) CHINA 6) FLOCK.
Cellar Doors 1) POTATO 2) CARROT
3) GRAPE 4) TURNIP.
GRAPE IS THE DOOR THAT LEADS
OUT, IT IS THE ONLY FRUIT.
Riddle - CROWS
Box Boggler Missing Letters - F, O, X
Animal - FOX.

28) Castle Snaps - 3 & 5 ARE THE SAME.

31) Quiz 1) OSLO 2) WORM 3) GALE
4) MOON. Word - BITE.
Three words - TRAP, BOWL, SMART.

32) Crossword Across 1) COW
3) NAP 5) MAY 6) EEL 8) PEA 10) HAT.
Down 1) CLOWN 2) WEB 4) PONY
5) MOLE 7) LAVA 8) PEACH 9) CAT.

33) Tug of War - MOVE THISTLE NUMBER
6, THEN BOTH SIDES WILL TOTAL 33.

34) Jig's Riddle - ELGIN.
Jag's Riddle - LOCHS.

35) Box Boggler - A, M, T = MAT.
1 TO 5 - LETTER T, TOP, STAR, STORE,
TOWS, POTATO.

37) Creature Quiz 1) B-FLOCK 2) B-EMU
3) A-CATFISH 4) C-CHICK 5) B-FOX.
How many legs = 20.

38) 1) BEAVER 2) AFRICA 3) GOLDEN 4)
PARROT 5) IGLOOS 6) PYTHON 7)
EIFFEL 8) SATURN.

39) Identical Photos B, W, L, O = BLOW.

40) Highland Fling - 1 + 6 ARE IDENTICAL.

RED ZONE

42) Hidden Bird of Prey - OSPREY. THE HUMMINGBIRD CAN FLY BACKWARDS.

43) Clusters - A=2, B=4, D=3, E=1. 'C' IS THE ODD ONE OUT.

44) Crossword DAY, BIN, EAT, CAR, ART, POT, HAM, WIN, YEA, EAR, MAR, BUT, ARK, WAS, ASH, OUR. Thistle - 9.

45) Zoo View - SEAL, WORM, SNAIL, MOUSE, LOBSTER, OSTRICH, SWAN, DEER, VULTURE, PENGUIN, TOAD, SLUG, TIGER, ROBIN, ROOK, LION.

46) Jar Switch - REMOVE THE JAR OF 18 ECLAIRS. THERE WILL THEN BE 53 ECLAIRS, 53 CARAMELS AND 106 TOFFEES.

47) Store Room BOX NUMBER FOUR. ALL ROWS DOWN, ACROSS AND DIAGONALLY ADD UP TO 20.

48) FROG, TIGER, ZEBRA, PIG, BEE, LION, LIZARD, CAT, COW, ALLIGATOR BEAR, OCTOPUS, CHICKEN, TURTLE, SNAKE, CROW, BUTTERFLY, SHEEP, DOG, TOAD, DEER, GOAT, EEL, MONKEY, ELEPHANT, RAT, SHARK, SPIDER, APE, GIRAFFE.

49) Missing Items - TELEVISION, TABLE, PICTURE.

50) Blockheads Blue BOILED, DRIVER, SILVER, BLINKS. Red SPRING, GRADES, MEDALS, STREAM. Boggle Squares 1) WINDOW, WIPERS, TASTES, WALLET. 2) BANNER, RELAYS, SPEAKS, BRANDS.

52) Place in Scotland - ELGIN. Famous Scot - BURNS.

53) 1) FALSE, SOUTH POLE 2) FALSE, A BOAT 3) TRUE 4) FALSE, ALASKA 5) TRUE 6) TRUE 7) TRUE 8) FALSE, A FISH 9) TRUE 10) FALSE, 8.

56) City Links AUSTRALIA-MELBOURNE, FRANCE-NICE, U.S.-WASHINGTON, ROMANIA-BUCHAREST, TURKEY-ANKARA, SPAIN-MADRID, EGYPT-CAIRO, GERMANY-HAMBURG,

PERU-LIMA, GREECE-ATHENS, ITALY-ROME, CANADA-TORONTO, ENGLAND-LONDON, JAPAN-TOKYO.

57) Triple Snap 1) BUBBLE 2) PACKET 3) WINDOW 4) CLOUDS

58) Fourteen Words, Across - VAT, PARROTS, SLATE, OPENS, BATH, CRATE, TWIG. Down - LAIR, TART, STOP, SET, EAR, OUT, SOW. Bat Wall A-8, B-11, C-5. EACH BRICK ON THE BOTTOM ROW IS THE TOTAL, OF THE TWO BRICKS DIAGONALLY ABOVE IT.

59)

61) Word not used in alphabet - DOT. Word not used in the grids - CAR.

62 & 63) Across 1) LIP 3) TEA 6) MOO 7) ARK 8) YEAR 10) SHUT 12) BEE 13) LES 15) COIN 16) CUB 17) MAY 18) MOTH 26) WIG 27) TWO 28) FRY 30) TAR 32) HUGE 33) WEAK 35) ILL 36) LAP 38) ASH 39) KEY. Down 2) PLUM 3) TALK 4) PONY 5) FAST 9) APE 11) HOE 12) BRUSH 14) STARS 15) CRABS 19) HAZEL 20) DAWN 21) JERRY 22) LOW 23) OAK 24) QUIET 25) WOOL 29) RUG 31) ACE 32) HULK 34) KILT 35) INCH 37) PINK.

64) Whailing Whale - Across COVERS, TRAVEL. Down OVER, ROPE.

65) 2+7 ARE THE SAME. Nine Words ROB, TAB, BEE, BUT, HUB, BOY, BAR, NIB, BYE. 6-letter word CAMERA.

67) 1) RUSSIA 2) ITALY 3) FRANCE 4) USA 5) GREECE 6) SPAIN 7) DENMARK 8) ARGENTINA 9) PORTUGAL 10) GERMANY.

We hope you enjoyed our Puzzle Book.
There are lots of interesting places to visit
throughout Scotland.
We would like to show you more, but we are
too busy trying to get our airplane back!
Hope to see you again!

Jig & Jag